MONTH-BY-MONTH

Arts & Crafts

DECEMBER · JANUARY · FEBRUARY

Compiled and Edited by Marcia Schonzeit

SCHOLASTIC
PROFESSIONAL BOOKS

New York · Toronto · London · Auckland · Sydney

To my son Sam,
a swell cutter and paster.

Designed by Nancy Metcalf
Production by Intergraphics
Illustration by Terri Chicko, Joe Chicko, and Stephanie Pershing

Cover design by Vincent Ceci
Cover photography by John Parnell

ISBN 0-590-49124-5

Scholastic Inc. has made every effort to verify attribution for each of these ideas. Scholastic Inc. regrets any omissions. The ideas were compiled from *Instructor* magazine.

CONTENTS

DECEMBER   7

December overflows with holiday spirit, from the first bulletin-board calendar to the last take-home goody bag! The month abounds with festive classroom decorations, gifts, ornaments, and cards that carry through Christmas and Hanukkah themes.

JANUARY   29

The year is off to a good start with winter projects that really warm up the imagination. Explore new techniques and new ways of using familiar materials. Remember Martin Luther King by making—and wearing—a dream T-shirt.

FEBRUARY   49

Celebrations begin with unique craft ideas for commemorating Presidents' Day, Black History Month, and Groundhog Day. Heartfelt Valentine's Day projects include suggestions for cards and carryalls, decorations and designs, and more!

Using This Book in Your Classroom

Month-By-Month Arts & Crafts offers you more than 50 classroom-tested, illustrated suggestions for every month of the school year. Because most of these projects were submitted to *Instructor* magazine by teachers just like you, you'll find them teacher friendly, success oriented, and appealing to a wide range of ages and abilities. Designed to promote individual creativity, the activities will please you as well as your students. Keeping in mind the needs of today's classroom, these art-and-craft experiences rely on inexpensive, easy-to-obtain materials. The emphasis is on simplicity, minimal fuss, and the fun of creating.

The activities, categorized by month, range from holiday decoration ideas in December to heart-warming Valentine's Day suggestions in February. Seasonal projects celebrate major holidays and highlight other special events every month. In addition, there are ideas for bulletin-board displays and class projects as well as opportunities to experiment with such techniques as collage, papier-mâché, painting, puppetry, and drawing.

Many of the projects also integrate other curriculum areas. Working out a quilt design, for example, or planning a class calendar involves mathematical concepts. Having students tell a story about their drawing establishes a language arts link. And social studies tie-ins occur naturally as part of activities that celebrate birthdays of inventors, presidents, and other national figures. Scientific principles are implicit in experiments with watercolor techniques or drawing from observation.

A resource section on page 70 suggests background information and sources of inspiration to spark projects from paper folding to creating papier-mâché angels and assembling collage compositions. Finally, the index presents activities in alphabetical order, with special listings for major holidays.

Evaluating an arts-and-crafts project is no longer limited to judging whether or not a child is "good" at art. More important is the expression of each child's unique view of the world. Experiencing the joy of seeing and the pleasure of creating are goals worth encouraging. Through these projects children learn to experiment without worrying about the "right" answer. They learn to expand their imagination. And they learn nonverbal ways to express themselves.

You may want to establish a link between school and home. A reproducible Letter to Parents on page 6 of this book enables you to enlist help from home in assembling scrap materials of all kinds. After your students have completed the activities in each of the *Month-By-Month* books, invite parents to an exhibition of the children's projects. Involve the class in displaying the artwork, taking home invitations and conducting tours through the gallery. Encourage home displays, too, with holiday gifts and other take-home ideas.

We hope that *Month-By-Month Arts & Crafts* provides you and your students with many hours of creative pleasure.

Letter to Parents

Teachers, you may want to make copies of this letter and hand them out to your students during the first week of school. You can save time and paper by highlighting the objects you need as the projects come up. Remind your students to return the letter with the material from home. Place the letters in a file until you're ready to send them home again. Don't write any names on them—that way you can redistribute them.

Dear Parent:

We need your help!

Our class needs the following items for our arts-and-crafts projects. Please start saving them now, and I'll let you know when we'll need them.

Due Date

1. paper towel rolls
2. toilet paper rolls
3. magazines
4. soup cans
5. pieces of cloth, fabric scraps
6. ribbons, yarn, string, rope
7. cardboard boxes
8. old greeting cards
9. paper plates
10. wire coat hangers
11. clean Popsicle sticks
12. other:
13. craft materials you'd like to share with us:

Thanks,

DECEMBER

From the bulletin-board calendar that marks the holiday countdown to the take-home goody bag, December is brimming with holiday spirit! Plastic straws, paper plates, cardboard tubes, and other common materials become uncommon gifts and decorations. Celebrate with snowflakes, reindeer, dreidels, and peace doves!

December Calendar

Students cut pictures from last year's holiday cards and paste them to the inside of folded sheets of red or green construction paper. Assign each person a December date; it is printed on the outside of the folded paper. Pictures and dates can be accented with glitter, sequins, yarn, and so on. Arrange folded sheets in sequential order on the bulletin board with only the date showing. As each date arrives, open the folder to show the picture.

Alicia Kazimir

Rag Wreath

Use all kinds of fabric scraps and ribbon for this festive project. Bend a wire coat hanger into a circle. Leave the hook on for hanging later. Cut material into 6- by 1/2-inch strips. Tie strips around the wire. Add a jaunty bow at the top.

Joan Mary Macey

Bulletin-Board Quilt

Make a bulletin-board quilt for Santa to rest under. Each child decorates a square with holiday symbols. Add a headboard and Santa's head asleep on a pillow.

Ruth Mugerauer

Miniature Evergreen

Let students grow their own evergreen tree. Remove stem of a pine cone so it will stand. Submerge in water, then remove and sprinkle evenly with grass seed. Put in a container with a half inch of water. Place in sunny spot. Water well and trim to emphasize shape.

Sharon Chamberlin

Light-Switch Santa

Cut a face for Santa Claus out of construction paper. Cut a 1-by-½-inch rectangle where the nose should be.

Cut a hat from red construction paper and glue to the top of Santa's head. Spread out cotton and glue on Santa's face for a beard. Spread out and glue on cotton for trim on hat as well. Let dry, then draw on Santa's facial features with crayons or markers.

Place Santa over a light-switch plate and attach to the wall with masking tape. Watch your Santa light switch brighten any room for the holidays! The light switch serves as Santa's nose.

Mary Ann Brensel

Tissue-Paper Windowpanes

Share the Christmas spirit with all who pass your windows. Cut snowflakes from folded black paper. Mount pieces of bright tissue paper behind them and fasten to the window with cellophane tape. Other Christmas symbols will be effective, too. Use the side of a short piece of chalk to make designs on black paper. Cut out spaces between the wide chalk lines. Remember that outlines should be connected with one another and with the outer frame.

DECEMBER

Holiday Glow

Fold a 9-inch by 12-inch piece of colored construction paper in half lengthwise. Draw a squiggly candle shape and cut out. Unfold and glue the candle to a 12-inch by 18-inch sheet of black construction paper. Add a flame cut from yellow or orange paper. Drip glue along and around the candle as well as emanating from the flame. Immediately sprinkle with gold or silver glitter.

Joy Lindner

Ornaments From the Sea

If you are near a source of seashells, turn them into tree ornaments. Children decorate them with tempera and add red yarn for hanging. (If shells do not already have a hole, use glue.) Put these shells on your class tree, then send them home for students to enjoy there.

Phyllis Scarcell Marcus

Dove of Peace

To make this graceful, white dove, you'll need a 9-inch paper plate, green construction paper, felt-tip markers, a green pipe cleaner, small white feathers, and glue. First, trace a dove profile and two wings on the paper plate and cut the shapes out. Glue the wings to each side of the dove and attach the feathers to the wings. Color in the eyes and beak. As a finishing touch, slide a pipe-cleaner olive branch through a hole in the beak, then glue on green construction-paper leaves. Attach yarn or string to the doves and hang in a pleasing display.

Sharon Zarka

Real Branch

Anchor a branch in a pebble-filled flowerpot, a poured plaster-of-paris block (use milk-carton mold), or a wide Styrofoam base. Trim with cut-paper ornaments, rich with glued-on glitter and colorful foil.

Holiday-House Ornaments

Punch holes in narrow top flaps of milk container, reglue flaps, tie string through holes to hang. Cover with foil; decorate.

Eleanor Hartmann

Paper-Plate Snowman

Use a paper plate to make this happy snowman! Draw a line around the perimeter of the plate, 1 inch from the outer rim, leaving a 2-inch segment blank at the top. Draw a concentric circle 2 inches inside the first line. Leave a 2-inch segment blank on this line as well, directly opposite from the first blank segment. Cut along the lines. Do not cut where the blank segments are.

After cutting, you will have three sections: one solid circle in the middle and two hollow circles on the outside. All three sections will be connected by the uncut segments. Fold the solid center section up to form the head. Fold the outside hollow circle down to form the lower part of the snowman's body. The middle hollow circle will form the middle of the snowman's body. Decorate the top circle with construction-paper features, hat, and scarf.   Marcia Wolfe

Rootin' Tootin' Twine Holder

Start with a cylindrical oatmeal, cornmeal, or salt box to make this useful and decorative gift for the entire family. With bands of construction paper, dress cowboy or cowgirl, in belted blue jeans, fringed chaps, and bright shirt. This figure not only hides a ball of twine under a broad-brimmed box-top hat, but also keeps a small pair of scissors handy in a holster for cutting the twine. The holster is fastened to the box with a paper fastener. A fastener inserted next to hole where twine is released keeps twine from being accidentally pulled and tangled.

Holiday Goody Bag

This goody bag is perfect for toting party favors, cards, and treats back home. Just add a cutout gingerbread man to the center of a decorated bag. Punch two holes through the top of the bag and slide a piece of red and green gift yarn or ribbon through the holes. Personalize the goody bag and add jingle bells for a festive touch.

Trillis Shrader

Miniwreaths

Cut cardboard into small wreath shapes. Glue on tiny pine cones, holly, dried or silk flowers, and other trimmings. Dry, then add cloth or yarn bows.　Renate Wehtje

Holiday Picture

Choose a holiday scene from a card or magazine. Paste toothpicks around it to make a frame. (An easy shape to use is a square with two more toothpicks pasted on top to form a peak.) Let the paste dry thoroughly. Carefully trim the picture away from the outside of the frame. Add two or four more rows on the peak to make it look like a roof overhang. Tape a yarn loop to the back and hang.

Jane K. Priewe

Triangle Tree

Cut two identical tree shapes from corrugated cardboard. Glue together with wooden dowel between. Cut, then glue lengths of green cellophane straws into the corrugations. Decorate with foil stars and balls.

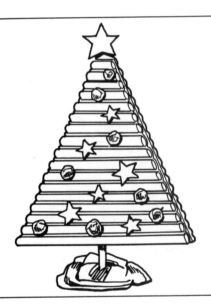

Paper-Plate Reindeer

Easy fun! Paste construction-paper eyes, nose, mouth, and antlers onto a paper plate. Glue to a dowel and use as a holiday reindeer mask.

Eleanor De Julio

Tissue-Paper Wreaths

To make each wreath, you'll need a package of green tissue paper, a few sheets of red tissue paper, a strip of red crepe paper, a wire hanger, scissors, and glue.

First, bend the hanger into a circle. Then cut the green and red tissue paper into 4-by-10-inch pieces. Fold a green piece of tissue in half over the bottom of the wire, twisting it two or three times. (Be careful not to tear tissue.) Slide the paper up to the top. Repeat this step with the rest of the green tissue paper, packing the pieces tightly together, until the hanger is completely covered. Occasionally weave in a piece of red tissue paper to form holly berries. Finally, fold a piece of green tissue paper into a narrow strip and wrap it around the bent hook at the top of the wreath. Secure ends with glue. Add a narrow strip of red tissue for a candy-cane effect. Finish with a big, red crepe-paper bow.

Norma Jean Byrkett

Paper-Circle Santas

Cut circles of various sizes from construction paper. Triangles can be used for beard and cap. Arrange, then paste together to make complete figures or heads. Add details of cotton, metallic paper, glitter, and so on. Use to trim packages or trees.

Clip-On Ornaments

Cut shapes from white paper and add details with colored paper or crayons. Glue the back of the shape to a wooden clip clothespin, making sure the bottom is close to the clip part of the clothespin. Clip to tree branches or to the ribbon on a wrapped gift.

Jane K. Priewe

Soft Sculpture

Cut doubles from fabric for each letter of a holiday word. Stitch together, leaving a small hole. Stuff, sew up, and assemble. Jay Scott

Freestanding Trees

Make a three-dimensional Christmas tree from green construction paper. First, have children draw two identical Christmas trees, as shown below.

Then decorate the tree with various pieces of Christmas wrapping paper cut into appropriate holiday shapes. After the tree is decorated, it can go home to add a festive note to children's bedrooms or play areas.

Straw Reindeer

Use two striped straws to make this decorative reindeer. Cut four body sections each 2 inches long; three 1-inch sections for a tail and head; and two antler sections each 1½ inches long. Paste the body sections together, side by side, and the tail section one-half inch below the back. Paste the two head sections together so that the top of the head is a half-inch above the back. When the paste is dry, slit the two antler sections lengthwise. Spread open, and cut two points on each side of the slit (antlers will curl). Use paste on the uncut ends and push antlers into each head section. Draw eyes, hoofs, and a nose with a black marker, and attach a string loop for hanging.

Jane K. Priewe

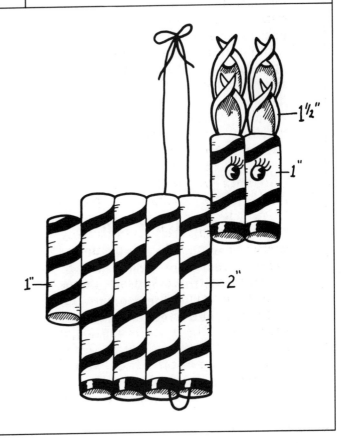

Rudolph, the Red-Nosed Puppet

Reindeer puppets delight young and old at Christmas. A 16-by-22-inch piece of paper is folded in half the long way. Fold once more to form a narrow, flattened tube. Tape the open sides together. Fold down top corners and tape. Next, fold entire top section down to make face. Add paper antlers, ears, nose, and bridle. Paint on other features and tie small bells to bridle.

Punch-Pattern Ornaments

Outline holiday ornament shapes on flat sections of foil pans and cut out. Sketch designs and punch along the lines with a nail. Ornaments can be left natural silver, antiqued with a thinned mixture of white glue and paint, colored with permanent markers, or painted in solid bright colors.   Jessamyn Williams

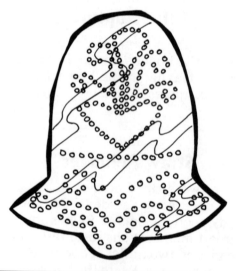

Christmas Tree Clips

Glue green felt to a small piece of heavy paper. Cut from the felt-paper a tree the length of a snap clothespin. Glue the tree to the clothespin, add a red-felt base, and decorate.   Jay Scott

Miniature Mobile

Cut tiny scenes from old Christmas cards. Mount on colored paper. Hang from decorated plastic cups with gold thread.

Doris D. Breiholz

Sponge Snowmen

Fold a sheet of construction paper in half and cut a snowman shape. Unfold paper and use as a stencil. Set atop another piece of construction paper and sponge inside the snowman shape with dabs of white tempera paint. Remove stencil and let dry. Use colorful fabric to add features.   Kathy Chandler

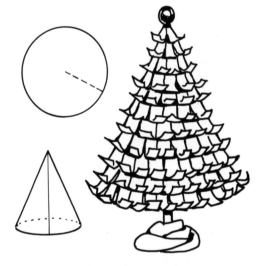

Cone Tree

Trim a stiff cone of sturdy paper or cardboard with strips of fringed or curled crepe, tissue, or construction paper. Or glue on various shapes of macaroni or cereal and then spray gold.

Santa Masks

Children can make a Santa Claus mask from construction-paper parts. First, have them cut a triangle from red paper and add a dab of cotton to the peak. Next, they glue a long sheet of paper to the bottom of the triangle for the face. Children cut out eyes, nose, and mouth and glue them to the face. Cut eyeholes. Next, they attach a 4-inch piece of white paper below the face for the beard. Children make three straight, vertical cuts (about 2 inches long) in the paper and curl the resulting strips around a pencil, as shown.

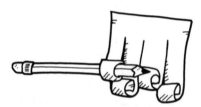

Children knot a piece of thin, lightweight elastic through holes punched in each side of the mask, and it's ready to wear.

Santa Sacks

On paper bags, add cut-paper decorations. For a 3-D trim, try a toboggan with a turned-up paper front, a paper-sculptured poinsettia, or a deer with velvet antlers. Use the finished bags to carry home Christmas-party goodies, or let them serve as wrappings for handsome gifts. Add paper handles, if you wish.

Sweet Rudolph

Paste a pompom nose and black felt eyes on the front of a candy cane's crook. Twist the middle of one pipe cleaner snugly around the peak of the crook to form part of the antlers. Cut a second pipe cleaner in half. Bend one of the halves to find the middle and twist around one antler to create three points as shown. Do the same with the second half on the other antler.

Jane K. Priewe

Eight-Sided Tree

Cut two identical tree shapes from tagboard. Slit one tree from tip to center; the other, from base to center. Fit trees together and decorate with yarn pompoms and small bows of yarn or rickrack.

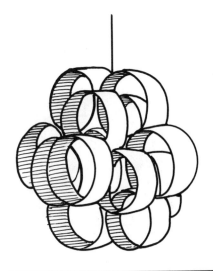

Artful Ornament

Cut small cardboard tubes into 3/4-inch rings, paint, and dry. Glue rings to form a pleasing design.

Jacqueline Koury

Sandymen

Sandpaper and paint can make wonderful holiday decorations for your classroom. Begin with an ordinary square of medium sandpaper. Draw or trace a gingerbread man shape on the back of the sandpaper and cut it out. Use white paint to add detail. Punch a hole in the top and attach thread to hang. The sandpaper gives a glittery, gingerbread look.

Newfield School Kindergarten Teachers

Christmas Stockings

Have children trace a stocking pattern on a "sandwich" of two sheets of red or green construction paper. Attach them together by stapling the sides and bottom or by lacing them. Children can paste an absorbent cotton border to the top front and add appropriate holiday designs. Children may want to add their names in glitter-on-glue: Print a name on the stocking and squeeze liquid glue over the letters. Immediately sprinkle glitter over the glue. (Be sure to place newspaper over the work surface so that children can shake off excess glitter.)

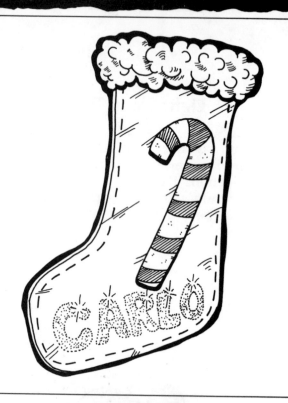

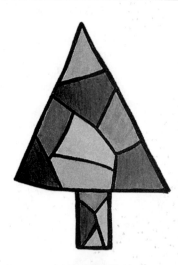

Stained-Glass Ornaments

With heavy scissors cut ornament shapes from the straight sides of plastic milk cartons. Color with transparent pastel markers. Outline the shapes and add features with black markers, using several coats so these lines are opaque. Hang in front of a lamp or in a sunny window. Jessamyn Williams

Spongy Snowman

Take the chill out of blustery winter days with this sassy snowman. First, tear around a sheet of black construction paper so that its edges are jagged. Then, using a sponge and premixed white paint, dab a snowman design on the paper. Add a jaunty yellow hat, eyes, carrot nose, big smile, and buttons from construction paper.

Julie Stempinksi

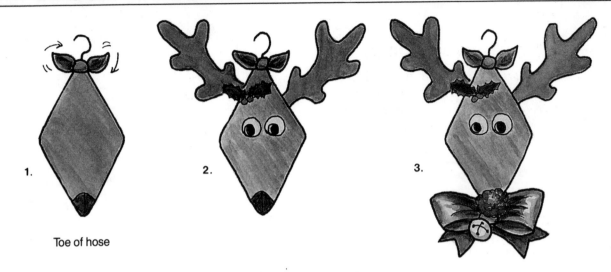

1.

Toe of hose

2.

3.

Reindeer Jingler

Bend a wire coat hanger into a diamond shape and cover it with the leg portion of an old pair of pantyhose. Knot the open end of the hose just under the hanger's hook to form reindeer ears. Make antlers from felt or construction paper. Glue on antlers, a red pompom nose, and moveable eyes. (Eyes and pompoms are available at most stores that carry sewing notions.) Add holly under one antler. Finish with a red bow and jingle bell at the reindeer's neck.   Pam J. Collier

Fabric Initials

Help children draw outlines of sister's or brother's initials on doubled pieces of bright-colored fabric. Letters can be equal or varied in height but not taller than 8 inches. Cut out initials and glue the two pieces together with a thin line of glue. Decorate with buttons, colored yarn, sequins, and so on. Great to hang on bedroom wall of brother or sister.

Jacqueline Koury

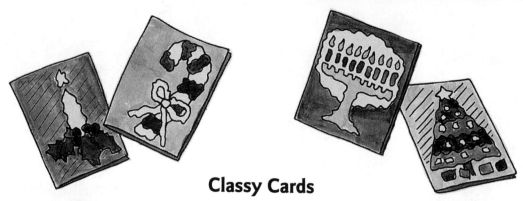

Classy Cards

Try this quick and easy torn-paper technique to create striking greeting cards. Gather the following materials: red, green blue, black, and white construction paper; white typing paper; and glue.

First, choose a holiday motif for the card, such as a candle, tree, wreath, menorah, dreidel, winter scene, snowman, candy cane, and so on. Fold a sheet of construction paper in half, then tear small pieces of construction paper into the shapes needed for the chosen design and glue them onto the construction-paper card. Next, fold a sheet of typing paper in half and insert it into the card. Secure with a few drops of glue. Add a personal holiday message inside. Happy holidays!

Sister Mary Roseen

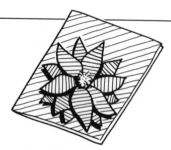

Perky Poinsettia Card

For each card, you'll need red and green construction paper, an index card, glitter, and glue. First, fold a sheet of green construction paper in half. Cut a circle from the index card and staple it to the front of the construction-paper card. Next, cut 10 to 12 petals from red construction paper and glue them, overlapping slightly, around the circle. Attach several petals to the underside of the circle to create depth. Apply glitter to the center. Write a holiday message inside the card and give it to someone special.

Beatrice Bachrach Perri

Holiday Postcards

Students can make holiday postcards to mail to parents and friends. Each traces around a standard postcard on heavy oaktag and cuts it out. Using crayons or felt pens, they draw holiday designs on one side. The card is then turned over and a vertical line drawn down the middle. A message is written on the left side, the address on the right. Add a stamp and mail.

Phyllis Scarcell Marcus

Holiday Handkerchief Holder

The cleverest way yet to give a handkerchief! Don't conceal it in a box, but display it as part of its own pretty package. Make a paper-tube Santa with construction-paper features and clothes, omitting arms. Cut off the tip of the cone hat and pull a bit of the hanky through to make a tassel. Slit the tube and pull through Santa's "beard" (the corner of the handkerchief). To remove handkerchief from the tube more easily, pin on hat with three straight pins.

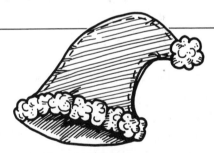

Santa Hats

Children can make a paper hat like Santa's by tracing this pattern on two pieces of red construction paper, cutting them out, and stapling the sides and top together. They can add "fur" trim made of white absorbent cotton or white felt. The children will enjoy wearing their Santa hats as they go caroling through your school or elsewhere.

Fern Christmas Tree

Earlier in the year collect ferns and dry them between pages of old magazines. When holiday time comes around, use rubber cement to glue each fern onto colored paper. Decorate the "tree" and use crayons and construction paper to add a surrounding scene. Cover with clear contact paper.

Ireene Robbins

Ring Around the Napkin

Cut cardboard tubes from paper towels or toilet tissue into 1-inch rings and wrap with colored yarn. Add designs by gluing holiday motifs cut from construction paper or fabric. Take home as a good family gift.

Marilyn Karns

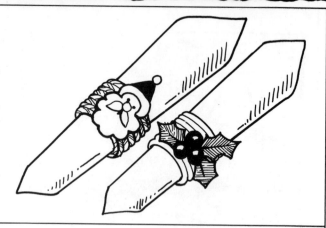

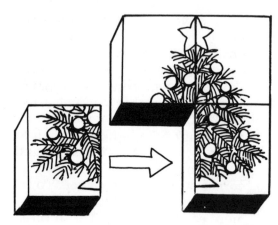

A Puzzling Present

Collect four small boxes just alike (perhaps the small laundromat detergent boxes). Cover on all sides with colored paper. Find a picture that fits area of the four boxes, fold in half both ways, cut along folds, and paste one piece on each box.

Diane Crane

Party Place Mats

Add a jolly touch to your class party with these whimsical holiday decorations. To make each place mat, you'll need a 12-by-18-inch sheet of oak tag, red and brown drawing paper, felt-tip markers, ribbon, and scissors. First, cut scalloped edges around the red paper and attach it to the center of the oak tag. Lay two strips of ribbon, one vertically and one horizontally, across the place mat. Glue down. Cut a gingerbread man from brown construction paper; draw on eyes, nose, mouth, and buttons. Print the child's name below the buttons. Paste the cutout to the center of the place mat, where the ribbons cross. Laminate if possible.

Trillis Shrader

Mâché an Angel

Angels are a part of nearly every religion—from Hinduism to Christianity, Judaism to Islam. Ask children to draw their conceptions of angels—how they look, what they do. Then create angels by rolling newspaper into a cone and stuffing with dry paper. Use tape to hold the "body" in position, and crush dry paper to make the head. Bunch up paper for wings and arms. Secure with tape.

Next, dip the torn strips into papier-mâché "batter." Cover each angel with two coats, smoothing out any bumps and holes. Allow two days to dry; paint, then poke a hole through the back of each one. Hang by a wire or string.

Another method involves briefly soaking a wad of newspaper in the mixture and shaping it by pulling an twisting. Smooth out and refine the features with additional dipped strips.

Marla Kantor

• *See page 70 for a book of picture references.*

Pine-Cone Angels

Glue a small nut on the tip of cone for head, and draw on features with fine marker. Use raveled yarn for hair, dried leaves for wings, pipe cleaner for halo and arms, golf tee or cake candleholder covered with foil for horn.

Elaine Scarpino

Miniature Piñatas

Children will love making their own Mexican piñatas. Collect small, sturdy boxes and help each child construct an animal. Place goodies and trinkets in the box. (Keep the side where the box opens on the bottom.) Cover with fringed tissue paper and add a face.

Jay Scott

Holiday Hang-ups

Cut holiday designs from packing cardboard, all shapes and sizes. Decorate with brightly colored tempera paint, plastic-foam packing "popcorn," or "slices" of paper tubing.

Doris D. Breiholz and Joan Mary Macey

Kwanzaa Cards

Design a card for Kwanzaa, an African-American harvest holiday celebrating seven principles: unity, self-determination, responsibility, cooperative economics, purpose, creativity, and faith. Each night, families light a candle, exchange gifts, and then discuss a principle.

Marilyn R. Reid

Delicate Holiday Cards

Use a paper punch to make aluminum-foil dots. Arrange dots on folded construction-paper cards and glue to create a menorah or other holiday symbol. Add candles and flames or other details with paper scraps or markers.

Beatrice Bachrach Perri

- *You may want to review with your students that Hanukkah is the Jewish Feast of Lights. It lasts for eight days, usually in December. It is a happy time when people give presents, sing songs, and play games.*

Hanukkah Goody Box

Make a gift box from a half-gallon milk carton. Cut curving sides as shown. Cover the sides with bright paper. Add symbols or other Hanukkah decorations and edge each side with pieces of yarn. This box is sturdy enough to hold cookies, a jar of apple butter, or other Hanukkah food gifts.   Marion Goldman

• *See page 70 for a Hanukkah picture book.*

Dreidel Cards

Cut a dreidel shape for a pattern. Students trace pattern on folded paper, with left edge of pattern on the fold. Cut out, but do not cut along fold. Using pattern, trace the shape on a single layer of calico or other fabric. Glue fabric to front of card with white glue and press until dry. On front of card glue a paper strip saying "Hanukkah" and write a short greeting on the inside.   Stella Simon

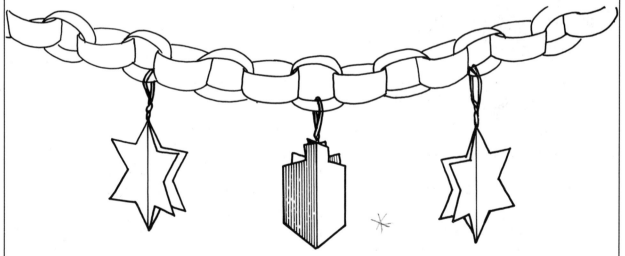

Hanukkah Chains

Make a paper-ring chain. Cut two dreidels from tagboard, fold each in half, and glue them together along the fold. Make a three-dimensional Star of David the same way. Hang dreidels and stars from the chain with thread.   Jay Scott

Hanukkah Cards

Fold a rectangle of construction paper in half. Glue on a simple construction-paper menorah. Add snipped paper straws for candles, bits of orange yarn for flames, and a greeting inside.

Jay Scott

Collage of Stars

In advance, prepare several equilateral triangles of varicolored construction paper, foil, felt, sandpaper, wallpaper samples, and so on. Children put two triangles together, one on top of the other, to make a Star of David, as shown.

Have children make several such stars from a variety of materials and paste them collage-fashion on a sheet of blue construction paper.

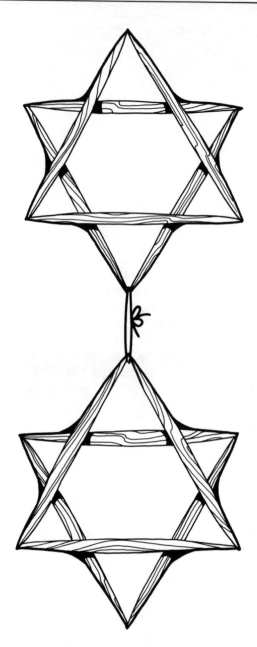

Hanukkah Mobile

Glue together toothpicks to make two equilateral triangles. Invert one triangle and glue it over the other to make a Star of David. Construct two or more additional stars. Suspend them with fine thread. Many mobiles hung in a line make a see-through curtain.

Marion Goldman

JANUARY

Warm up with winter projects that really fire the imagination! Paint a poem, experiment with scrap-box art and a batik technique. Other craft suggestions include a bird feeder, oak-tag sculptures, and a dream T-shirt to make for Martin Luther King Day.

Calendar Creations

Let a giant calendar be the focal point of your room. Square off a chalkboard into correct number and arrangements of days for current month. Or draw calendar on large paper and tape it to the bulletin board. Space for each day should measure at least 4- by 6-inches. Each child designs, letters, and tapes up an assigned day. Weather, historic events, or important incidents in children's own lives can be recorded.

Clever Clocks

To remind children that time is measured not only in minutes and hours, but also in days, weeks, and years, have them design a decorative clock in a case. The clock face is a recessed paper plate (taped from behind) with movable hands attached with a paper fastener. A small calender is worked into the decoration at the base of clock. Use wood-grained wallpaper for this project, if it is available.

Toast the New Year!

Have children write New Year's wishes on decorated strips of writing paper about 1 inch by 8 inches. Each student will need a paper or Styrofoam cup to decorate with markers or crayons. Exchange wish strips by giving children time to deposit wishes in one another's cups. Take turns reading wishes aloud, fill everyone's cup with punch, and drink a special toast to each other and the new year.

Ann Gediman

Resolution Sled

Trace a sled pattern on construction paper. Print a New Year's resolution on the top or on a runner. Cut out, decorate, fold runners down, and display as a fun reminder.

Doris Meyer

New Year's Resolutions

After discussing New Year's resolutions, have each child make a personal list. From these lists, students choose one to use on a cut-paper T-shirt. Fold white paper in half, sketch a neck opening (along the fold) and the sleeve and side areas, then cut along these lines. Write and illustrate the resolution, and hang on cord.

Talis Byers

Dream T-Shirts

Dream T-shirts let children wear their hopes for all to see. Don them to celebrate Martin Luther King, Jr. Day.

To make Dream T-shirts, ask each child to bring in a plain, cotton T-shirt. Remind students that it was King's dream that all people be given the freedom to realize their dreams. Suggest students illustrate their own dreams on the front of their shirts. On the back, they can list steps they'll take to achieve their goals.

Two tips: Place sheets of cardboard inside the shirts to keep colors from bleeding through as children decorate. Try waterproof markers or acrylic paint and the dreams will be indelible.

Barbara Ellis

• *See page 70 for background information on Martin Luther King, Jr.*

Dream Cakes

Crayons and paper are all you need for children to make the layer cakes of their dreams. Have students design a cake for someone special and write their wishes for that person in between the layers. Your whole class can make a huge cake on poster paper to give to the principal or learn about Louis Braille, Jacob Grimm, Horatio Alger, Jr., and other birthday celebrants this month. What might be appropriate wishes for them?

Susan Rodriguez

Paint a Poem

Try this activity on a snowy day. Give students paper and paints, then read this poem aloud. The imagery is sure to inspire some originality.

Snowfall
The giant shears his woolly sheep
On the moon one winter night
And the downy fleece
that falls to earth
Makes a blanket soft and white.

Beverly McLoughland

Feathered Friends

Birds of all species—cardinals, bluejays, blackbirds—may be represented like the one in the illustration. Cut the head and body of the bird from construction paper. Add some details and fan-fold matching tissue paper for a tail. Glue or staple together at one end and glue to the bird. Cut tissue paper twice the tail length for the wings and fan-fold lengthwise. Cut a slit in the bird and insert pleated tissue halfway; fold back on each side and glue the edges against the body.

Patricia Wilmott

Winter Wonderland

Have a classroom drive for any kind of white odds and ends—cotton swabs, plastic egg cartons, packing pieces, textured fabrics, buttons, straws, cotton batting, tissues, yarn. Let children make a selection and create a white scene on a dark paper background.

Kathleen Decker

It would be wonderful to be able to grow...

49¢

Balloon Bushes

Directions: Needs hot air, colorful climate, and blue skies.

CAUTION: Do not plant next to Cactus.

their writing

My fantasy garden would be filled with ... this Spring

Fantastic Seeds

Students can create their own special seeds. All you need is paper, scissors, glue, uncooked rice, and markers. Discuss all the things it would be wonderful to be able to grow, and have each child decide what he or she might like in a fantasy garden—anything from balloon bushes to a rainbow tree. Seed packets should include an illustration of the full-grown "plant," planting information, and garden hints. Provide a pattern from a seed packet, help children fold paper into an envelope shape; decorate, insert rice to simulate seed, and seal. Encourage children to use their imagination.

Susan Rodriguez

Oak-Tag Sculpture

Before you suggest this sculpture project to the children, prepare a large number of one-inch-wide paper strips cut from oak tag. The strips should be of at least three different lengths—6 inches, 9 inches, and 12 inches.

Tell the children you want them to make some building squares. They do this by folding each strip in half and then folding it in half again. To form each square, one child can hold the loose ends of each strip, while another child tapes them to form a neat corner.

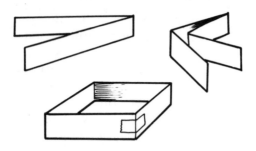

Have each child make 18 such squares. That should supply plenty of building squares for each sculptor.

Next, the sculptors go to work—stacking, spacing, and balancing. As the squares are placed in position, they should be taped together at the points where they meet.

Encourage the children to let their imaginations run free. Who can make the tallest sculpture? the thinnest? the widest? the most top-heavy? Who wants to add color to his or her sculpture? As a sculpture "grows," it may need to be supported on a piece of thin cardboard. (Extra oak-tag building squares could also be used as manipulatives during math activities.)

Calendar Catchall

Cut a paper plate in half. Attach one half to a whole paper plate for a pocket. Decorate, then fasten a small calendar to the pocket. Attach yarn and hang.   Barbara Ellis

A Winter Scene

Have upper graders draw bare trees on pastel paper. Next, they tear shapes of black hills and white snow banks. On separate paper they draw, color, and cut out an animal. Finally, they arrange all pieces in front of the trees.

Sister Gwen Floryance

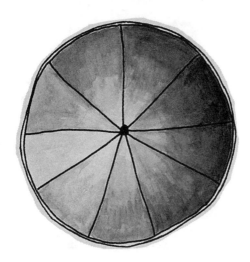

Wheel of Color

Older children can make their own color wheels. Use pencil to draw a large circle on oak tag and a ruler to divide it into nine sections. Paint any one of the sections red, skip two sections, and paint the next one blue. Skip two more and paint that section yellow.

Next, fill in the empty sections with paint mixed from the two colors on either side. The yellow-orange shade should be in the block next to the yellow and the reddish-orange color next to the red. Continue around the circle mixing colors: Put reddish purple and bluish purple between the red and blue; blue-green and yellow-green between the blue and yellow.

Children can experiment by adding small amounts of white and black to the colors in each section. Sections can be divided into strips so that lighter color moves toward the center and darker color toward the edge. As students perfect their mixing techniques, they may want to create more complicated wheels, with subtler shades.   Marla Kantor

- *See page 70 for a book about color.*

Scrape-Box Art

Scrap-box art provides instant inspiration for a quick, imaginative art project. Have each child choose one scrap from a box of leftovers and then paste it in any position on a plain background paper. Next, have the children turn the paper in every direction. What does the scrap look like—a person, object, animal? Use crayons to define and complete the picture.   Dorothy Gordon

Oil Slicks

Draw a design with a felt-tip marker on white paper. Outline with markers of other colors. Brush with water. Mount on black paper.

Stained "Glass"

With a black marker, draw a winter object or design on acetate. Fill in, using brightly colored markers. Cut out, attach a string or thread, and hang in a sunny window for winter cheer.

Jay Scott

Stamp Pictures

Save cancelled stamps from discarded mail. Soak in water to remove from envelopes and wrappers. Paste stamps of the same color in groups on scrap paper. Cut into desired shapes. For a 3-D effect, paste corners of old envelopes onto collage and trim into open cuplike forms (for flowers, hats, or house roofs).

Tony Hall

• *Don't forget that January is Stamp Collectors' Month!*

Monkey on a Stick

Children never tire of hearing stories about monkeys and will enjoy making their own little monkey climbing on a tree branch. Take wooden ice-cream sticks and glue them together vertically by overlapping the edges. Use white glue. Allow the sticks to air-dry. Have children draw or trace a monkey shape onto brown construction paper. Students cut out the monkey and draw in facial features with colored markers. Glue the monkey on the stick. Cut leaves from green construction paper and glue onto each side of the stick to look as if the monkey is climbing a tree.

Sally Jarvis

Inventions

Have each child cut out two circles, triangles, and rectangles (from colored paper, gift wrap, wallpaper, foil, etc.). These shapes form the basis for an imaginary vehicle. Children glue the shapes to construction paper and add finishing details with crayons.

Pincushions

Cut a 4-inch circle of heavy material and stretch it over a ball of steel wool. Push the covered steel wool through the center of a canning ring. Glue a canning lid underneath to hold padding in place. Trim ring by gluing on strands of beads, rickrack, pieces of lace, or fancy ribbon.

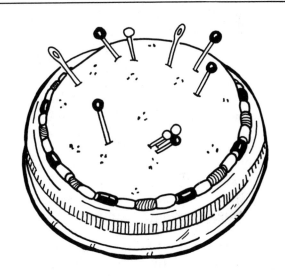

Whatchamacallits

Have children bring in scraps from home, including yarn, buttons, cans. Contribute colored paper, tissue paper, and any interesting art items you can find. Then let children's imagination do the working. Have students design their own "Whatchamacallits," name their new creations, and create their own exhibit.   Linda Martin Mercer

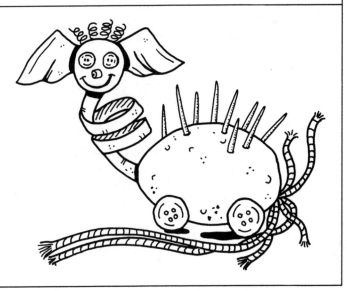

Papier-Mâché Zoo

Start with the idea of creating a grand zoo, jungle, or circus. Roll dry newspapers into cone or tube shapes to make basic animal bodies. Use masking tape to hold the shape in place. For example, create a tiger with a tubelike body of rolled newspaper. Use tape to fasten on smaller tubes for legs.

Mix the flour and water in a bowl to a creamy oatmeal consistency, and tear additional newspapers into long, thin strips. Students can work in pairs, dipping strips into the mixture, removing excess "goop," and covering the entire beast. "Squeeze" a wad of dry newspaper to make a head and secure it with tape and more wet strips. For ears and a tail, use the strips like tape to secure small paper wads.

For an alternative "skeleton," experiment with plastic containers and cardboard tubes. Tape the pieces together, then use the same method to papier-mâché. Make sure each animal is sturdy, with at least two coats of strips.

Animals take about two days to dry, then on to the painting! With a good selection of tempera colors, imaginations will soar. Books on folk art and crafts add inspiration.

Marla Kantor

Touch-Me Art

Primary children love to learn about animals. Start saving rug scraps, fabric, feathers, and yarn now, to help them create their own. After you have talked about various creatures, let children "build" the beast of their choice. Encourage adding little extras such as tails made of feathers and pipe-cleaner whiskers. You might even want to provide plastic eyes.

Loree Spuhler

Winter Bouquet

Cover a paper cup with patterned paper. Then fold green construction paper in half lengthwise. Cut into folded edge halfway across the width to create a row of stems. Roll entire paper lengthwise to bunch stems, then place in cup with stems facing up. Paste flowers on stem ends for a beautiful winter bouquet.

Ruth Belgine

Bag Houses

Each child draws lines on an empty bag to create three "floors." With tempera students add doors, windows, and so on; stuff with crumpled newspaper; staple shut and add construction-paper roofs.

Carol Hutchinson

What Color Is Your Imagination?

Find a story, fairy tale, or vivid poem to read to your class. Tell children that they are illustrators and should choose the section of the story they "see" as the most colorful. Have students add details verbally, then translate these details into a drawing of the scenes as they visualize them. Crayons and oil pastels are perfect tools for such drawings.

Encourage individual insights into how characters look. Explain there are many ways to draw a horse, many kinds of saddles, blankets, and bridles, full of colors and decorations. Talk about the many different ways a face can look, different details such as freckles, a beard, a long craggy nose that add to the character of a face. Discuss that when pictures originate from the imagination, each one will have its own unique look.

Marla Kantor

• See page 70 for source material to spark imaginations.

Wax Paper Snowflakes

Cut wax paper into 5-inch squares and give two to each child. Hold the square together and fold them in half; then fold in half again. Cut out interesting curves on the two open sides. On the folded edges, cut out small holes, triangles, or other shapes, making sure to keep the edges connected. Open the snowflakes and place them one on top of the other, rotating one at a 45-degree angle. Press the pieces together with a warm iron (have an adult do this). When cool, hang the snowflake from the ceiling or in a window with a piece of string.

Angela Andrews

Space Art

For stars, dip toothbrush in white paint and flick onto black paper. On another sheet of plaper, paint planets. While wet, sprinkle on tempera powder to create "craters." Cut out and glue to star background for an original version of the universe.

Batik Made Simple

Crayon resist is an old favorite that children delight in. Start with white or colored paper, but not black. Students draw any subject in crayon on the paper. When each drawing is complete, the child covers the entire surface with watered-down tempera paint. Black creates a dramatic effect, but any color or combination of colors can be used. Wherever there is crayon, the paint will "resist" adhering but will fill in the noncrayoned areas.

This technique is a simplified version of batik. In batik, hot wax is applied to fabric, then the fabric is dyed. The wax resists the dye, then is later ironed out, leaving the design. To most closely replicate batik, draw with a white crayon on white paper, then paint; only the white crayon will show through.

Marla Kantor

Sun-Fades

Give each child a piece of manila or white drawing paper. Students draw and then cut out a simple shape such as a butterfly, flower, car, animal, airplane, or rocket. Staple this shape (one staple will do) to a piece of brightly colored construction paper. Tape paper to the window, with the cutout shape next to the glass, facing out. Leave the sheets up for about two weeks. When you take down and remove the shapes, the sun will have faded the paper all around them, but the shapes will stand out in all their glory.

Bettie Walker

Drawing From a Viewpoint

Exercising the imagination is easy for some children and difficult for others. Encourage students to take a point of view when drawing. For instance, a beach scene looks different to the lifeguard at the top of a tower than it does to a sunbather sprawled on a towel. Even a ladybug in the garden sees the hoe differently than the gardener does.

Snowmen

Use plastic trays, paper plates, doilies, and cotton to make original snowmen. Tall figure A is made from three plates, one slightly larger than the other two. Plastic trays and boxes made the tubby man B, and cotton, figure C. Scraps of colored paper, buttons, and cloth become eyes, noses, mouths, and clothing. Mount completed people on construction paper and surround them with crayon or chalk snowdrifts.

Marcia Wolfe and Ireene Robbins

Snowman Poem:
My feet are cold
My nose is, too.
But my heart is warm
With love for you.

Making Moonscapes

You will need a 9-inch cardboard circle for each child, tongue depressors, India ink, watercolor brushes, lightweight aluminum foil, assortment of junk objects (chunks of cardboard, wads of discarded foil, nuts, bolts, screws, bottle caps, heavy cord), and masking tape.

To introduce this project, ask these questions: What does the surface of the moon look like? Are there mountains and craters? Who can describe one? The surface of the moon is full of interesting textures. We are going to create a kind of textured surface that will be exciting to look at as well as to touch.

Then ask students to tape a pleasing arrangement of objects onto their cardboard circles. (See illustration.) When they are satisfied, have them place a piece of foil over the cardboard; starting from the center, press the foil closely around each raised form, working out to the edges. Excess foil at the edges can be folded tightly and taped to the underside. Then brush India ink over the entire surface. When dry, each child can use a tongue depressor to gently scrape off the ink from the higher areas, leaving a dramatic textured pattern.

As students are finishing, you may want to ask these questions: Who is ready to show us his or her moonscape? What are some of the objects you chose to create your moonscape? Did anyone discover an interesting way to crease the foil to create more textured effects? Do you like the effect of the India ink? How does it provide contrast to the foil?

Janet Carson

• *See page 70 for other art activities to help children communicate.*

Zipper Art

Combine a collection of odd zippers with paper, glue, and dozens of different answers to the question, "When is a zipper not a zipper?" The answer shown here is, "When it looks like a decorative dog collar." Zippers can also appear as mouths and traditional closures for handbags, pillows, boots, and other items of clothing.

Ireene Robbins

Winter Night

Cover a bulletin board with black paper. Add white paper cut to look like drifting snow. Make houses with colored paper and marking pens. Tiny gold stars "light" the scene. Edge the board with cotton.

Mary Cobb

Picture Starters

You can stimulate young artists with "picture starters" similar to the story starters that are used in writing projects. Proposing "situations" to draw as a way of motivating young children can be very successful.

For example, second graders were told to use crayons and draw a bunch of balloons at the very top of their paper. After they had done this, they were told to imagine themselves attached to the balloons, being carried away up and over anything they wished!

Calico Cats and Gingham Dogs

It's off to a whimsical start by reading aloud Eugene Fields' well-known poem, "The Duel." Follow with a discussion of the terms *calico* and *gingham* and show fabric samples of fine prints and checks.

Allow children complete freedom to design their own versions of the animals in the poem. Some may wish to make actual stuffed animals. Others might use wallpaper prints to cut out flat figures. Real fabric can be pasted to paper plates with wallpaper paste. Finished animals would make spritely decorations for children's bedrooms at home.

Snowless Snowman

Give children black construction paper, clear-drying glue, and instructions to make a snow sculpture from the materials in the classroom hodgepodge box. In the box put packing foam, yarn, and facial tissue. Colored paper adds interest.

Eloise Riner

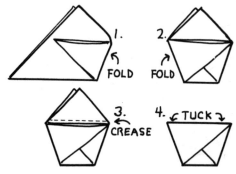

Folded-Paper Cups

Take a square of paper and fold it in half diagonally to make a triangle. Fold each bottom point up to the opposite side. Crease the top triangles and fold each down, tucking the front one inside to hold it all in place. You have made a paper cup that will hold water nicely!

Fran Stallings

• *See page 70 for books that include other paper-folding projects.*

Snow Scenes

When students feel restless, let them draw snow scenes on the windows with shaving cream. Give each child a squirt of foam to use for fingerpainting. When the shaving cream dries, wipe it off with a cloth.

Ellen Javernick

Winter-Sports Figures

Form figure skeletons from rolls of newspaper taped together. Or use a medium-weight flexible wire (or pipe cleaners) padded with cotton. Wire will allow figures to bend freely and show better action. Use cloth, tissue, and crepe paper to dress figures. This might be a good time to discuss the importance of dressing suitably for the weather.

Travel Game

Wash and dry the molded clear plastic bubble that wraps luncheon meats. Place on heavy cardboard and trace around it, adding 3/4 inch. Draw and color a picture on this cardboard. Poke holes to hold small beads and glue bubble over the cardboard. Tilt the game to roll beads into holes.
Jane K. Priewe

Crayon-Ironing Variation

Here's a new variation on an old idea. Substitute erasable bond typing paper for art paper. Place two pieces of paper together with small pieces of crayon between them. Students iron the paper with a warm iron (make sure there is adult supervision). While the sheets are warm, students pull them apart. Many interesting colors and textures result. Paste onto construction paper for display.
Julie Stempinski

Portrait Plates

Students might enjoy designing caricatures on paper plates. These may be well-known figures in story-books, history, current events, or even the cartoon strips. Make a "Guess Who We Are" bulletin board with answers concealed in envelope tacked in center of board.

Purr-Fect Cats

Make a very small hole in center of an oatmeal box lid. Cut string 2 feet long, push through the hole, and knot on the inside of the lid so it won't pull through. Glue lid to box and cover with orange paper. Glue cat shape to the box, tail end toward string. Draw thumb and first fingernails down the string to make kitty "purr."   Jeff Hart

Experiments With Watercolors

To experiment with color shades and tones, have students paint with color complements (colors across from each other on the color wheel such as red and green. Add varying amounts of black to one color to change tone, and use adjoining colors on the color wheel to experiment with color families.

Encourage children to try over-lapping brush strokes using one or several colors so strokes are un-detectable and create painting washes.

Give students a chance to prac-tice brush strokes, noting the dif-ferences between a wet or a dry brush, a pointed or flattened tip, thick or watery paint.

Another method is lifting paint by blotting damp or redampened areas with tissues, sponges, or towels. Move paint with the edge of a piece of cardboard, or sprinkle the paper with salt or sand to ab-sorb moisture.

Cut favorite experiments into shapes and mount them on a solid color background.

Collage Ingredients

Choose three or four "main ingredients" for this collage—paper tubing, plastic straws, macaroni, and yarn could be one group; seashells, twigs, unusual papers, and sand, another; magazine pictures and print, a third. Also provide two or three colors of paint for children to use as another element in their collage. This project develops a sense of design and discrimination. It's also interesting for children to compare what others do with the same set of materials. Marla Kantor

• *See page 70 for source materials to use with collage projects.*

Bird-Feeder Fun

For a feeder that withstands bad weather while it attracts the birds, start with a quart-size tin can, two wooden spools, two aluminum-foil pie pans, and some yarn. Remove the top of can and punch openings all around bottom edge. Put a small hole in center of each pie pan and in bottom of can. Thread parts together with several long strands of yarn. Finish off at bottom with a large knotted tassel to help draw the birds' attention. Fill feeder by sliding up the top spool and pie pan. Decorate can with painted birds.

 ## Newspaper City

Students cut building shapes from classified sections of newspapers. Include churches, schools, stores, municipal buildings, and so on. Arrange and glue on a plain background. Add watercolor washes and line drawings to provide architectural details, trees, and vehicles. Celeste Bouchillon

FEBRUARY

Celebrate Groundhog Day, Black History Month, and Presidents' Day with unique craft ideas. Eagles, log cabins, and presidential portraits turn up in a wide variety of materials on cards, banners, and bulletin-board displays.

Valentine designs range from teddy bears to lovebirds and include clever paper-cutting ideas and suggestions for colorful mobiles.

Liberty Bells

In February, when we honor U.S. presidents, it is fitting to discuss the time when America gained her liberty and independence. Students can make small liberty bells to remind them of the people and events that shaped our country.

Use a nut cup for the bell, a piece of knotted rope for the clapper and, for a holder, cardboard taped to the cup. Paint bell and clapper gold, and add a "crack" with black paint. Or suggest that students design original liberty bells from larger paper cups and decorate with patriotic symbols.

Home Sweet Burrow

Fantasy can be a wonderful addition to your art program. My students exercised their creative imaginations by drawing their ideas of Mr. Groundhog's underground home. This is a February activity with a decided difference! A classroom discussion can encourage imaginative "house plans." Children will enjoy sharing their designs.   Marilyn Carden

• *See page 70 for books to share on Groundhog Day.*

Presidential Eagles

Bits of colored tissue paper were used for this small mosaic eagle. A larger one could be made with torn pieces of colored magazine ads or wallpaper.

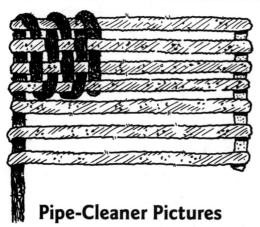

Pipe-Cleaner Pictures

Children who excel at manipulative skills do not always feel confident with drawing and painting. Give them the opportunity to "draw" or "design" with pipe cleaners instead of the penciled or painted line and you may see an amazing change in their responses. You can emphasize February's patriotic aspect by limiting work to a red, white, and blue color scheme. Try feestanding motifs as well as gluing the designs against flat backgrounds.   Joan Lunich Schenk

Lincoln and Washington

Lincoln and Washington actually served our nation some 64 years apart, but their names are irrevocably linked in the minds of most children. Let your class draw these two February patriots together in a star-spangled scene that makes liberal use of the colors red, white, and blue. Students can check reference books to make sure details are accurate.

James Perrin

Penny Pendants

Each child traces and cuts out a 2½-inch red circle, a 2-inch white circle, and a 1½-inch blue circle and glues them together—blue on white, white on red. Glue a new penny in the middle of the blue circle. Add white yarn for wearing around the neck to celebrate Lincoln's birthday or Presidents' Day.

Vi Johnson

A National Eagle

Eagle is cut from two stacked plates glued at center but not at rims. Scallop and cut apart fluted rims for feathers, and glue these on body. Fold top talons forward, bottom ones backward, so bird can stand.

Cherry Tree Time

George Washington and the tale of the cherry tree seem to be inseparable. So, use this well-known lore as subject matter for a free-expression art period. Let children engage in any art activity that can be related to the story. Some may want to design yarn-stitchery cherry trees. Others may wish to create paintings or dioramas that depict the much-described scene.

- *See page 70 for books to broaden your Presidents' Day celebrations.*

Lincoln's Log Cabin

Make replicas of long-ago log cabins from commonplace items of today, such as milk cartons and brown paper bags.

Use a pint-size carton or cut top from a quart carton. Glue a folded piece of paper to the straight strip at top of carton and paste sides of paper to slanted sides of container top. Form strips of paper (the same length as sides of carton) into "logs" by rolling strip around a pencil and pasting down its outside edge. Slide gently off the pencil. Glue logs to carton. Add a cardboard chimney, doors, and windows. Dab places where the light-colored container shows through (roof peaks especially) with brown tempera.

Heads of State

Pay tribute to your favorite president and celebrate Presidents' Day with this fun project. Each student will need one L'eggs® egg and the cardboard base package the plastic egg is sold in. Cover the plastic egg containers with clay. Sculpt features and glue on plastic wiggly eyes sold in craft stores. Or glue on a piece of hosierty for facial tone. Then cut features from felt or other material and glue to the egg. Roosevelt's glasses are made from a bent pipe cleaner. Use material or cotton for the presidents' hair, or add different-colored clay. The cardboard packaging is used for a base. Decorate it to look like a body, using felt, fabric scraps, or paper to make clothing. You now have a bust of your favorite president!

Marlene Goodwin

Foil Designs

Cover a piece of cardboard about 8 inches by 12 inches with foil. Cut such symbols as a liberty bell, Statue of Liberty, bald eagle, and so on from tissue paper and glue on the foil. Overlapping adds interest.

Evelyn Hill

Hall of Fame

Have each student choose one president and make a paper person of him. Students take home lengths of paper and trace around fathers or other male adults. Faces are done freehand or copied from the opaque projector. Research will reveal interesting clothing styles. Display completed figures around the classroom in honor of Presidents' Day.

Lincoln Figures

Lincoln makes a picturesque personage for children to create in 3-D, using a tin can as a base. His black beard and tall hat help to make him easily recognized.

Bold Eagles

Our national emblem, the eagle, has long been a favorite subject of designers and needleworkers. It has appeared on seals, coins, and flags, as well as quilts, rugs, and embroidered wall hangings. The eagle also makes a fine motif for soap carvings, mosaics, fabric stenciling, or paper sculpture.

The textured front section of the paper sculpture shown here is made of small brown squares folded diagonally, with one half glued to the background. Imagine a very large version of this on a bulletin board!

Lincoln Profiles

After studying some "penny views" of Lincoln, have children make silhouettes on oak tag and cut out carefully, leaving the outside for a stencil. Place stencil on paper and tape at edge to prevent slipping. Pat a paint-moistened sponge around opening and then fill in center.   Annie Burns Hicks

3-D Plaques

Outline identical circles on the front of one paper plate and on the back of another. Draw Lincoln's profile in the circle on plate back. Fill in with black paint or marker and cut away the rest of the circle. Paint or paste stripes and stars in circle of other plate. Glue rims together.   Jacqueline Koury

Black History Collages

Make black history come alive with this bulletin board that reinforces social studies and art. First, have each child choose a famous black American, past or present, and pick several important aspects of the person's life to research. (For example, if a child chooses Ella Fitzgerald, he or she might do research on jazz.) Next, have students make 9- by 12-inch collages using magazine-picture cutouts to represent their chosen person. Place the collages on the bulletin board. Follow up by having students give brief oral presentations in character, then have them take turns interviewing each other.   Charlayne McLeod

Black Hero Portrait

Draw portraits of black American heroes on drawing paper. Add color and background with watercolors. (If the paint is too thick or thin, the portrait will wrinkle as it dries.) Dry on a flat surface, then mount on colored construction paper.   Doris Alexis

- *See page 70 for background materials for Black History Month.*

African Gourd

Thoroughly clean an empty one-gallon liquid laundry soap container. Allow to dry completely. Then use felt, markers, macrame beads, or whatever is desired to decorate. Fill with bells, beads, or gravel for a musical sound when tapped.   Barbara Ellis

Valentines With Streamers

Give children two shades of valentine-colored construction paper from which to cut two of the same sized pieces (as pictured). Weave the pieces together and staple or paste to finish off. Attach all sorts of streamers with shiny paper hearts to hang from the ends. Write valentine messages in interesting places.   Joan Mary Macey

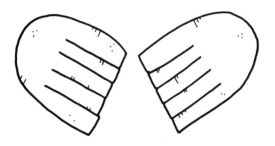

A Heartfelt Quilt

Have students draw all kinds of hearts: elongated, squat, curvy, silly. Fill each in with many colors: Maroon on the bottom, reddish-orange across the middle, peach on top, another in shades of blues and violets. Put three to five of these hearts in carious positions on each card and color the background, too.   Marla Kantor

• *See page 70 for ideas to inspire valentines.*

Flowery Valentine

Cut heart with top on fold so card will open for inside message. Cover front with flowers cut from seed catalogs, magazines, or gift wrap. Overlap so that no background shows. Paste on letters naming recipient.

Gail Baer

Teddy Bears

Children love teddy bears! Draw a picture of a teddy bear on a 9- by 12-inch piece of construction paper. Color in the picture. Cut a T-shirt from felt or material and glue onto the teddy bear. The teddy bear's "fur" is wood shavings collected from the class pencil sharpener and neighboring classroom sharpeners. Apply these wood shavings like glitter. Simply cover teddy bear with glue, sprinkle on shavings, and shake off excess into wastebasket.

Beatrice Bachrach Perri

Valentine Banner

Plan banner first on paper before cutting from felt. Cut paper design apart and pin on felt for pattern. Cut out with sewing scissors. Assemble with any fast-drying white glue. Use a dowel or tightly rolled paper for hanging rod. Be sure to leave enough empty space at top of banner for rod pocket.　Julia Brown

Valentine Letterbox

Cover each side of a tissue box (4¼ by 5¼ inches) with colored paper. Do not paper over the top opening. Decorate with valentine symbols cut from paper or fabric. Glue a paper doily around the top opening so children can use the box to store valentines.

Valentine Animals

When this art project is finished, your bulletin board will have a menagerie of heart-warming and lovable animals. Begin by having children cut out many, many hearts of different shapes, sizes, and colors. Then students arrange and rearrange them to make their creations. They can use hearts of many colors and draw in some of their animals' features. When satisfied with their finished animals, students glue or tape the hearts together to make them permanent. Display animals on a bulletin board covered with white paper and trimmed with red rickrack.

Rosiata Gonzales

Valentine Designs

Use hearts of all colors in ths valentine display that combines positive and negative areas. Notice how one heart is upside down and cutout centers are used as parts of the design in other places.

Arthur B. Kennon

Secret Admirer

Create a colorful name disguise. Have children fold paper in half lengthwise and use a dark-colored marker to print their name in large block letters. The fold is their bottom line. Next, fold paper inside out, hold up to window, and trace letters to wrong side of paper. Fold paper back to original position and trace name again so that letters finally fall opposite the first printing. Color in all the empty spaces so the letters become a design.

C. R. Fivver

Valentine Rainbow

Cut a circle of paper the same size as the center of a lace doily. Design a heart and rainbow to fill the circle. Color with markers. Glue in center. Then color certain parts of the doily edge. Cut away other pieces to make the edge more interesting. Mount on paper and fold in half for a card.

Mary Wright

Have-a-Heart Quilt

Give each child an 8- by 10-inch piece of construction paper; half the class has red, half white. Students then decorate their paper rectangles with small hearts, valentine messages, and their names. Cut a large heart shape from tagboard and glue each rectangle on the heart, patchwork quilt style.

Fran Pelly

Valentine Kites

For room-brightening valentine decorations, you can't beat a collection of valentine kites. Let children think up their own ideas for designs and paint them on large red, pink, or white construction-paper kite shapes. Brainstorm for suitable sayings, such as "Love is in the air," to letter somewhere on the kites. Use string and crepe paper, tissue paper, or cloth scraps for tails. Mount kites high on walls around room.

Eileen Etna

Textured Tributes

Encourage children to make each valentine a "many-textured thing" by supplying a good variety of materials. Save candy-box papers, ribbon, buttons, beads, scraps of lace, gummed seals and labels, and leftover Christmas baubles. Have different shapes of macaroni available, making sure that the alphabet type is included. Gift-wrapping papers and a wallpaper sample book are fine additions, too.

Kitty Letterbox

Use a large-size detergent box. Tail and ears are cut from a paper plate rim. Ears are glued to another plate for the head, which is painted red. Glue on drinking-straw whiskers and cutout features.

Helen Morgan

Valentine Faces

Heart-shaped faces with heart-shaped features and curled- or shredded-paper hair make appealing valentines. Pieces of paper-lace doilies can serve as collars or hats. Real ribbon makes realistic neckties and hair bows. No two designs will be alike, so be sure to save time for an exhibition at end of class. Children will want to see and admire others' efforts.

Valentine Party Favor

At your class valentine party, pass out a sweet surprise that students then use to make a valentine favor. Fill fluted paper cupcake liners (use two for added strength) with small heart candies, and stick a lollipop upside down in each one. From pieces of red, white, or pink paper, children cut heart-shaped sails and flags, then slit them to slide over lollipop sticks. Red yarn "rigging" completes the small valentine ships.

Wall of Hearts

Heart minimurals are a good way for students to experiment with watercolor washes. Give each student a 12- by 18-inch sheet of white construction paper. Dampen the paper and dab on dots or stripes of paint, allowing colors to run together. When dry, draw five to eight heart silhouettes on the paper with a black felt pen. Cut the hearts out and leave a small border around the black outlines. Mount them in a row on a strip of heavy tagboard or matboard. Tie the design together with a border.

Carol J. Flatt

Friendship Stick

These keepsakes make lovely valentine gifts—with wishes wrapped into every part! Each child needs a stick—a branch, a wide dowel, or a long cardboard tube. Students wrap sticks with colorful string and yarn. They glue down one end of the yarn and begin wrapping. As each piece of yarn nears its end, children glue it to the stick a few inches from the yarn end. To hang "charms" from the dangling yarn end, children tie on feathers, shells, beads, paper hearts, or pipe-cleaner roses.

Sliding Valentine Message

On center fold of large paper heart, cut four horizontal slits about an inch apart, one above the other. Open heart and weave a constrasting strip of paper through the slits. Pull paper down to expose two blank areas at the bottom, then letter exposed areas of paper with a message. Decorate with cutouts.

Gail Baer

Valentine Holders

These happy valentine holders are made by cutting a lovable pet out of strong and heavy paper. Add features and glue or staple on a large heart pocket, leaving the top open for cards.

Sue Kreibich

Open Your Heart

Mark the center of a sheet of paper by lightly folding in half. Unfold and fold both ends to center. Cut two identical on-the-fold hearts. Cut one in half along the fold. Glue the uncut heart inside the card. Glue the halves on the front and tie the card shut with yarn.   Beatrice Bachrach Perri

Heart Designs

These rainbow-hued hearts make an uncomplicated, eye-catching valentine design. You can make your heart multicolored, or choose a very pale shade of one color and work outward to the darkest hue of the same color; or reverse the order and use the deepest shade in the center of motif. It may be necessary to paint some shades. Glue to the cover of a valentine card.

Mary Wright

Cupid Carryall

One and one-half paper plates, a length of yarn, and colored paper make this valentine carrier. Paint or paste Cupid's features and hair on one plate. Staple or stitch half-plate behind face to form a pocket for carrying valentine cards home from school. Insert cutout paper wings between plates before stapling. Attach yarn handle and carryall is done!

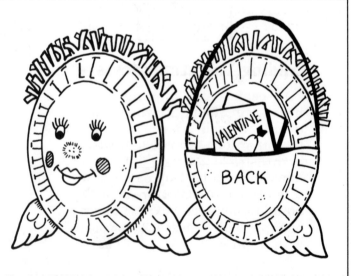

Puffy Valentine Card

Here's a three-dimensional card to give to someone special this Valentine's Day. For each card you'll need a sheet of construction paper, two pieces of heavy oak tag, a scrap of red fabric, cotton batting, pink and green crepe paper, and a paper doily. First, fold the sheet of construction paper in half and place a sheet of white paper inside. Then glue cotton batting to a heart-shaped piece of oak tag, cover with red fabric to create a puffy heart, and attach to the front of the card. Create a border with the doily and trim with crepe paper. Add crepe-paper flowers to each corner of the card. Write a personal message inside the card.

Christine Jensen

Valentine Greetings

Create old-fashioned cards with this traditional technique. Fold red paper in half, draw and cut out design. Cut motifs that are not on the center fold first. Use pointed scissors and cut carefully. Unfold and mount on white paper.   Lee Hall

Cord Heart

Twist together two equal strands of wrapped wire or long pipe cleaners. Form a heart shape and tie ends together. Decorate with colorful ribbons. Hang with ribbon.

Barbara Ellis

Valentine Display

Have each student cut out four different-sized hearts: one large red heart, two medium-sized pink hearts, and one small white heart.

Next, carefully pour white paint into a flat tray and have students take turns dipping one hand into the paint. To absorb excess paint, blot hands on a paper towel. Press their hand on the large red heart. Let dry.

Glue one pink heart to the left of the red heart and one to the right. Using a black marker, have children write the words "my," "stops," "4" and "U." Glue the remaining white heart next to the word "my."

Have students display their messages in the classroom or in the school lobby.   Jeannette Ramsden

Dove Note

The body of this white dove is a 2-inch tube of strong paper. Wad one end of a paper handkerchief and push into tube. Fluff the rest to form tail. Cut head from paper; fold one-half inch at the base of neck and paste to wadded end of paper handkerchief protruding from tube. Cut wings from paper and paste to body. Cut a heart-shaped base for dove and print valentine message on it. Or, cut a small heart and put greeting on one side, fold it in half, and slip it under one of the dove's wings.

Valentine Basket

Decorate a paper-plate half with valentine pictures or cutouts. Then staple two plate halves together at sides after rim handle has been inserted. To make basket stand up, fold bottoms of plates outward in opposite directions and staple them to cardboard. Cut to fit.

Cut-Paper Valentines

Fold a 12- by 18-inch sheet of white or red paper lengthwise two times. Make scissor cuts along the folds at intervals of about 1 inch. Do not cut any pieces of paper away. Cut along the entire length of the two edges, then open and glue or tape to a larger paper in a contrasting color.

Aileen M. LeBlanc

Valentine Memories

A few days before Valentine's Day, have upper graders make small booklets with as many pages as there are students in the class. At your valentine party, they can write couplets, haikus, limericks, or other poems in each others' books. Older children will enjoy creating this keepsake.

Lucinda L. Klevay

Heart Bugs

Children will love making their own "heartbugs." Let children put them together from a collection of small boxes, plastic-foam balls, shallow cans, pipe cleaners, lace, ribbon, fabric, and paper. Jody Owens

Have-a-Heart Bears

Cut out a teddy bear shape from brown corrugated paper and mount it on a square of cardboard. Make paws and a nose from scraps of felt or velvet, and all other features—including a big, warm heart—from scraps of colored paper. Add the words "Teddy bears his heart for you" to the creation, and send it as a valentine to a friend or relative.   Joan Mary Macey

Salty Heart

Use salt paint to decorate valentines. Mix four cups salt, one cup water, and one cup liquid starch in a large bowl. Stir well. Divide mixture into several containers with a different tempera color in each. Each child paints his or her heart as desired.   Kathleen Allan Meyer

Lovebirds Letterbox

Tape equal-sided carton shut and cover sides. Draw, paint, and cut out lovebirds on perch. Paste birds on one side and a cutout heart on each of the others. Glue yarn "bars" at regular intervals. Add decorative paper strips at top and bottom. Cut roof slightly larger than carton; base is covered cardboard.   Peggy Lin

Old-Fashioned Valentine

For each card you'll need a sheet of construction paper, tissue paper, a sheet of white drawing paper, colored markers or crayons, and glue. First, fold the tissue paper into a square or triangle and make small cutout designs around the edges and at the fold lines of the tissue paper. Fold the construction paper in half and attach the tissue paper to the front. Then cut the white drawing paper in half and attach it to the inside of the card. Afterwards, read Elizabeth Barrett Browning's poem, "How Do I Love Thee," to the class. Have children write Valentine's Day messages inside the cards.

Sarah Horton

Bookmark Hearts

Encourage students to put their hearts into reading with these Valentine bookmarks. Fill a shallow pan with water, then have students use scissors or vegetable peelers to scrape pieces of colored chalk into the water. Lightly stir the water to create patterns. Next, have students dip heavy drawing paper into the mixture. Remove and let dry. Outline heart shapes using cookie cutters, then cut them out. Use rubber cement to attach the hearts to strips of construction paper. Punch a hole through the top and attach an 18-inch length of satin ribbon as a finishing touch.

Norma Jean Byrkett

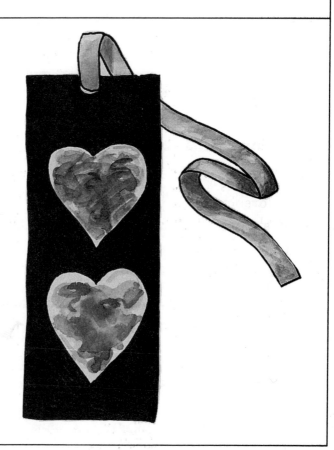

Resources

Paper Folding

Books that include other paper-folding projects:
Elementary Art Games and Puzzles by Florence Temko (Parker/Prentice-Hall, 1982)
Paper Dreams by Lorraine Bodger (Universe Books, 1977)

Hanukkah

To help explain how and why Hanukkah is celebrated:
A Picture Book of Hanukkah by David A. Adler (Holiday House, 1982)

Collage

Source materials to use with collage projects:
Pictures of the work of Romare Bearden, Arthur Dove, Joseph Cornell, Henri Matisse, and Kurt Schwitters
Picture books illustrated by Leo Leonni and Ezra Jack Keats

Angels

A picture-filled reference book:
Angels by Peter Lamborn Wilson (Pantheon, 1980)

Color

A sourcebook on personal interpretation of color:
The Art of Color by Yohannes Itten (Van Nostrand Reinhold, 1973)

Imagination

A book of visual poems by a painter:
Sounds by Wassily Kandinsky (Yale University Press, 1980)

Art Activities to Help Children Communicate

Tell Me About Your Picture: Art Activities to Help Children Communicate by Janet Carson (Prentice-Hall, 1984)

Martin Luther King, Jr.

Background for Martin Luther King Day:
I Have a Dream: The Story of Martin Luther King by Margaret Davidson (Scholastic Inc., 1986)
Martin Luther King Day by Linda Lowery (Carolrhoda Books, 1987)

Valentine's Day

To get into the mood for Valentine's Day:
Hearts, Cupids, and Red Roses: The Story of Valentine Symbols by Edna Barth (Clarion Books/Ticknor & Fields, 1974)
Valentine for a Dragon by Shirley Rousseau Murphy (Atheneum, 1984)

Groundhog Day

Storybooks to share:
It's Groundhog Day! by Jeni Basset (Holiday House, 1987)
Wake Up, Vladimir by Felicia Bond (Harper, 1987)

Presidents' Day

Facts, anecdotes, and offbeat information:
Facts and Fun About the Presidents by George Sullivan (Scholastic Inc., 1987)
The Last Cow on the White House Lawn by Barbara Seuling (Doubleday, 1978)

Black History Month

Nonfiction to share:
Freedom Train, The Story of Harriet Tubman by Dorothy Sterling (Scholastic Inc., 1987)
The Story of George Washington Carver by Eva Moore (Scholastic Inc., 1990)

Index